Mice and Rats

CHELSEA CLUBHOUSE

An Imprint of Chelsea House Publishers
A Haights Cross Communications Company
Philadelphia

June Loves

Chelsea Clubhouse
1974 Sproul Road, Suite 400
Broomall, PA 19008-0914

The Chelsea House world wide web address is www.chelseahouse.com

Library of Congress Cataloging-in-Publication Data

Loves, June.
    Mice and rats / June Loves.
    v. cm. — (Pets)

    Contents: Mice and rats — Kinds of mice — Kinds of rats — Parts of mice and rats — Young mice and rats — Choosing pet mice and rats — Caring for pet mice and rats — Cleaning — Feeding — Grooming — Handling — Training — Visiting the vet — Pet mouse and rat clubs — In the wild.

    ISBN 0-7910-7551-6
    1. Mice as pets—Juvenile literature. 2. Rats as pets—Juvenile literature. [1. Mice as pets. 2. Rats as pets.] I. Title. II. Series.
    SF459.M5 L68 2004
    636.9′352—dc21

                                                                    2002155669

First published in 2003 by
MACMILLAN EDUCATION AUSTRALIA PTY LTD
627 Chapel Street, South Yarra, Australia, 3141

Associated companies and representatives throughout the world.

Copyright © June Loves 2003
Copyright in photographs © individual photographers as credited

Page layout by Domenic Lauricella
Photo research by Legend Images

Printed in China

Acknowledgements
The author and the publisher are grateful to the following for permission to reproduce copyright material:

Cover photograph: girl with pet mouse, courtesy of ANT Photo Library.

ANT Photo Library, pp. 1, 4, 13, 25, 26; Kathie Atkinson/Auscape, p. 10 (top); Frank Woerle/Auscape, p. 30 (top); Australian Picture Library/Corbis, p. 30 (bottom); Getty Images, pp. 8–9 (main), 27; Legend Images, pp. 14 (brush & shovel), 15 (wood shavings); Lloyd Franklin, p. 29; MEA Photo, pp. 14 (chews), 15 (carrier & grooming brush), 18, 19; Pelusey Photography, pp. 5, 10 (bottom), 11, 14–15, 23; Photography Ebiz, pp. 6, 7, 8 (left), 12, 16–17, 24, 28; Dale Mann/Retrospect, pp. 20, 21, 22.

With special thanks to Annie and Rose of Oakleigh Pets and Food Supplies, the Tunstall Square Pet Shop, and to the Pets Paradise store in Doncaster Shoppingtown.

While every care has been taken to trace and acknowledge copyright, the publisher tenders their apologies for any accidental infringement where copyright has proved untraceable. Where the attempt has been unsuccessful, the publisher welcomes information that would redress the situation.

Contents

Mice and Rats

Mice and rats can be clean, friendly pets. They need their own houses with plenty of space. They are excellent pets for people who live in small houses or apartments.

Pet mice like to climb and play.

Pet rats are larger than pet mice.

Pet mice and rats need fresh food, water, and loving care every day. Mice are playful, interesting pets. Rats are quieter, intelligent pets.

Kinds of Mice

There are many **breeds** of pet mice. White mice are popular pets. Mice can be other colors, such as pink, cream, chocolate, silver, blue, or cinnamon. There are also **piebald**, striped, and spotted mice.

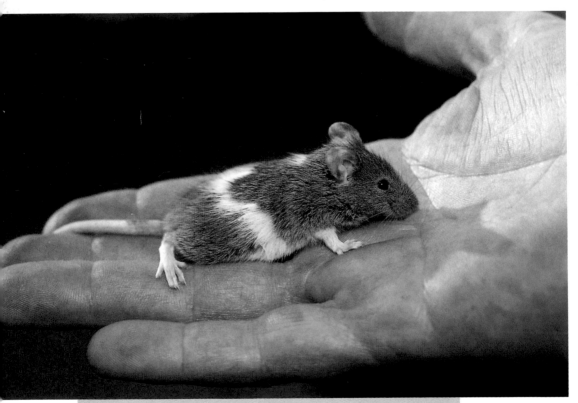

Some mice have markings such as stripes or spots.

Kinds of Rats

Pet rats come in different colors, such as black-and-white, black, chocolate, gray, or red. Albino rats are white with pink eyes.

Black-hooded rats have black coloring on their heads.

Parts of Mice and Rats

Mice and rats are **mammals**. They have the same body parts, but mice are smaller.

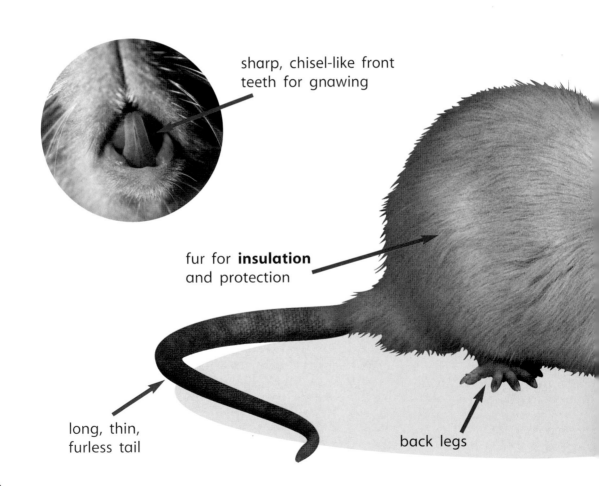

sharp, chisel-like front teeth for gnawing

fur for **insulation** and protection

long, thin, furless tail

back legs

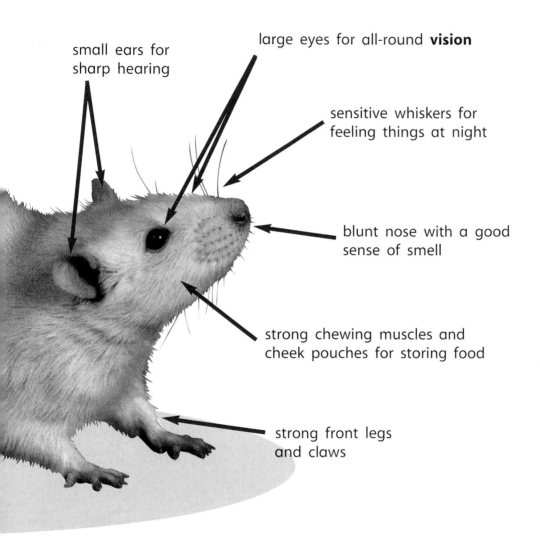

small ears for
sharp hearing

large eyes for all-round **vision**

sensitive whiskers for
feeling things at night

blunt nose with a good
sense of smell

strong chewing muscles and
cheek pouches for storing food

strong front legs
and claws

Young Mice and Rats

Female mice and rats can have from one to twelve young in a **litter**. When young mice and rats are born, they do not have fur, and their eyes and ears are shut. They feed on their mother's milk.

Newborn mice are helpless and need their mother.

Mice grow soft fur within a few weeks.

Young mice and rats are called pups.

Young mice stop feeding on their mother's milk after three weeks. They are ready to explore the world.

Mice can look after themselves when they are six weeks old.

Choosing Pet Mice and Rats

Choose pet mice and rats with shiny, clean fur, and bright eyes. Active, curious mice and rats make the best pets. Check that the cages where you buy your pets are clean and tidy with no smell.

Pet mice and rats can be held gently.

Pet mice and rats are ready to leave their mother for a new home when they are about six weeks old. Pet mice and rats like company. Think about keeping two pet mice or two pet rats.

Female mice get along well together. Male mice may fight each other.

Caring for Pet Mice and Rats

Prepare a house for pet mice and rats before you bring them home. Rats and mice need the same kind of home. These are some of the supplies you need to care for your pet mice and rats.

large, comfortable mouse or rat house

litter tray

brush and small shovel to clean up droppings

heavy bowl for food

hard items for chewing on

A piece of natural wood for chewing stops mice and rats' teeth from growing too long.

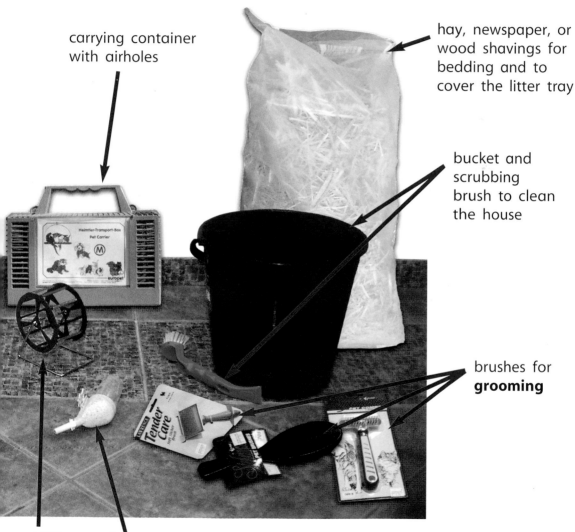

carrying container with airholes

hay, newspaper, or wood shavings for bedding and to cover the litter tray

bucket and scrubbing brush to clean the house

brushes for **grooming**

toys

heavy bowl for water, or a drip-feed water bottle

Pet mice and rats' houses

Pet mice and rats need large, escape-proof houses. Their houses should give them shelter and keep them safe from other animals.

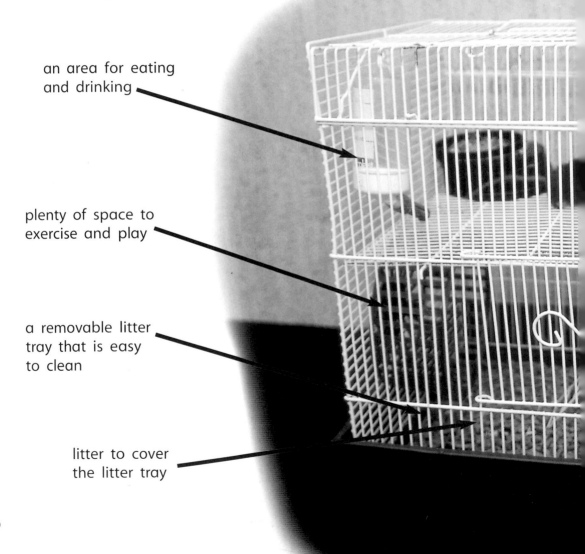

an area for eating and drinking

plenty of space to exercise and play

a removable litter tray that is easy to clean

litter to cover the litter tray

Pet mice and rats' houses need a dark area for pets to sleep in during the day.

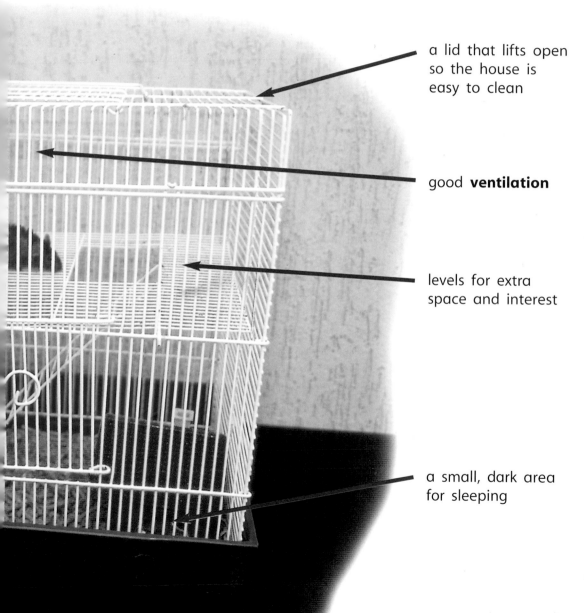

a lid that lifts open so the house is easy to clean

good **ventilation**

levels for extra space and interest

a small, dark area for sleeping

Toys

Playing with a variety of toys will give pet mice and rats exercise.

- ✪ Ladders, ramps, ropes, swings, and platforms are for climbing and swinging.
- ✪ Exercise and spinning wheels are for fitness.
- ✪ Hard plastic toys, twigs, and mazes are for exploring.
- ✪ Hollow logs and tunnels are for running through and around.

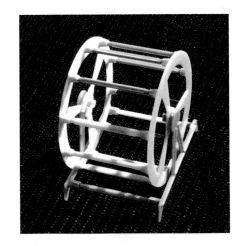

Toys will keep pet mice and rats happy in their homes.

Cleaning

It is important to clean pet mice and rats' houses every day.

The litter tray
✪ Wash and clean the litter tray every day.
✪ Replace the litter.

Food and water containers
✪ Clean food and water containers every day.

Use a sponge or brush to clean the litter tray.

The house

Make sure your pets are safe while you clean their house.

✪ Take out dirty bedding and uneaten food every day.
✪ Clean the house every month with warm, soapy water.
✪ Rinse and dry the house well.
✪ Replace the bedding, food, and water.

Wash the inside and outside of the house.

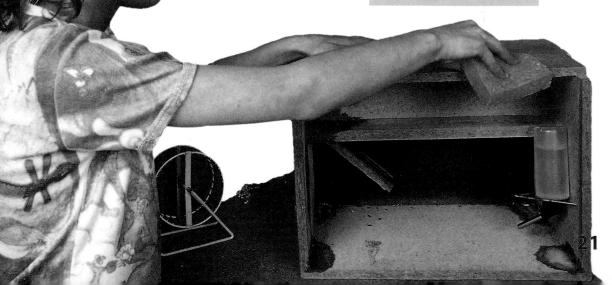

Feeding

Pet mice and rats need to be fed every day. You can buy mice and rat pellets from a pet store or supermarket. Store food in an airtight container to keep it fresh.

Pellets are the main part of a pet mouse or rat's diet.

Vary your pets' diet by giving them small amounts of fresh fruits, leafy vegetables, **root vegetables**, and grains such as bran, corn, or uncooked oatmeal.

Make sure your pet mice and rats always have clean water.

Grooming

Pet mice and rats groom themselves. They also enjoy grooming one another. You will need to brush and comb long-haired mice and rats gently.

Pet rats and mice bathe themselves.

Handling

Handle pet mice and rats gently. Most pet mice can be picked up close to the tail and placed onto your palm. Never pick up rats by the tail. Use both hands and support the rat's feet.

Cup your hand to hold your mouse safely.

Training

Mice and rats are clever pets. They can be trained to do tricks. Reward pet mice and rats with food and praise when you train them.

You can train pet mice and rats to sit on your shoulder or run up and down your sleeves.

This rat is finding its way through a maze.

Pet mice and rats can be tamed easily. If you gently stroke your pet, you can tame it to sit on your finger. You can also train pet mice and rats to find their way through a maze.

Visiting the Vet

If your pet mouse or rat does not seem well, take it to the **vet** for advice and treatment. A regular check-up will keep your pet healthy.

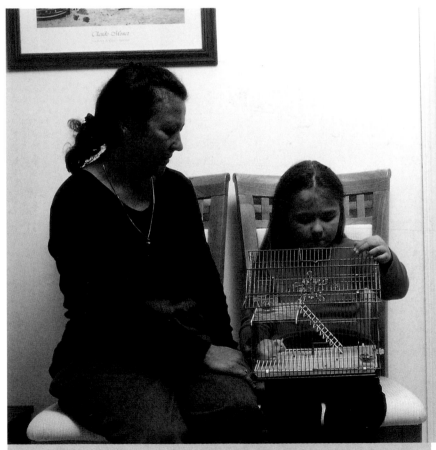

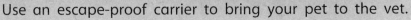
Use an escape-proof carrier to bring your pet to the vet.

Pet Mouse and Rat Clubs

Pet mouse and rat owners can join clubs. Pet owners meet to share information, have pet competitions, and join in fun activities.

Owners enjoy talking to others about their pets.

In the Wild

Many kinds of rats and mice, such as water rats and harvest mice, live in the wild. Water rats live near water. Harvest mice are very small and live in the open.

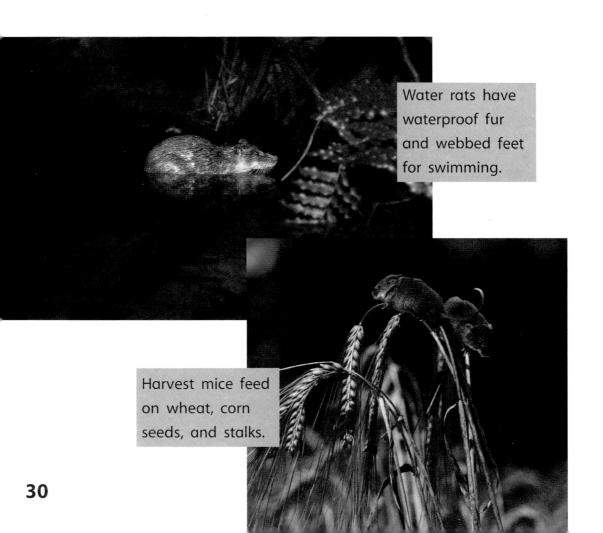

Water rats have waterproof fur and webbed feet for swimming.

Harvest mice feed on wheat, corn seeds, and stalks.

Glossary

breeds	animals that belong to the same scientific group and have a similar appearance
grooming	brushing or combing a pet to keep it clean
insulation	a way of keeping heat and cold in or out
litter	animals born at the same time to the same mother; also, a material used in a litter box to absorb waste and droppings
litter tray	a tray where pets can wet and leave their droppings
mammals	warm-blooded animals covered with hair whose young feed on their mother's milk
piebald	black-and-white patches
root vegetables	vegetables with roots you can eat, such as carrots and parsnips
ventilation	a way of letting plenty of air into a place
vet	a doctor who treats animals; short for veterinarian
vision	ability to see

Index